Summer Is Here!

By Jane Belk Moncure

Illustrated by Frances Hook

THE CHILD'S WORLD
ELGIN, ILLINOIS 60120

Library of Congress Cataloging in Publication Data

Moncure, Jane Belk.
  Summer Is Here!

  SUMMARY: A child relates the enjoyable character-
istics and activities of summertime.
  [1. Summer—Fiction. 2. Stories in rhyme]
I. Hook, Frances. II. Title.
PZ8.3.M72Su   [E]   75-12945
ISBN 0-913778-12-5

PICTURE WORDS

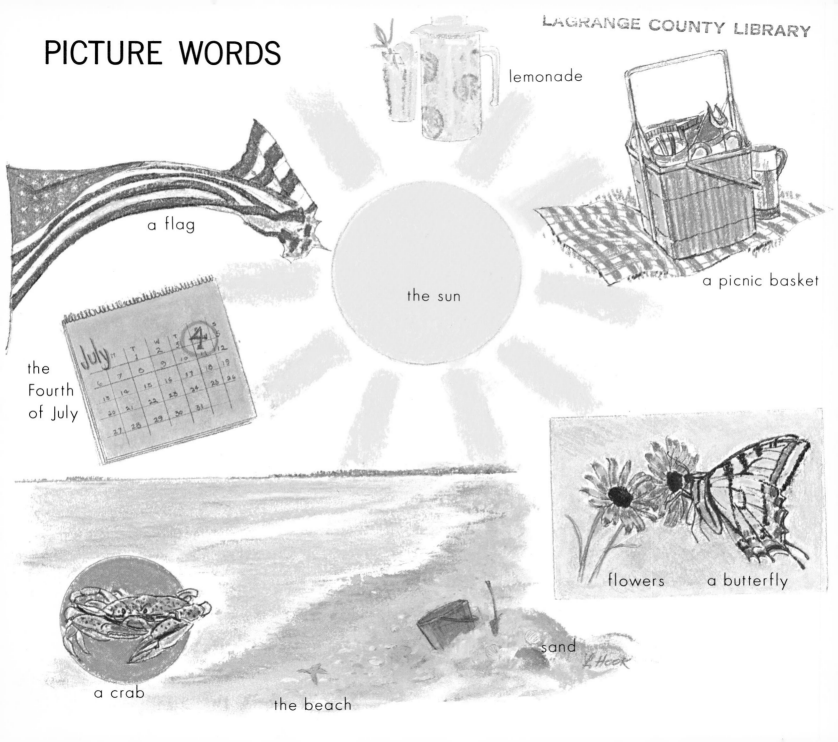

lemonade

a flag

a picnic basket

the sun

the Fourth of July

July

flowers   a butterfly

a crab

the beach

sand

I like summer.

Come and play.

Today is a summer holiday.

Flags are flying in the sky.

People say, "Happy Fourth of July!"

Wave your flag and kick your feet
   as we go marching down the street.

I like summer.

I like a parade.

March in the sun.

March in the shade.

March to our store and

drink lemonade.

I like summer.

I like to go to the fields
where the summer flowers grow.

I talk to a butterfly, but he
is much too busy to talk to me.

Sometimes it rains on a summer day.

Rain, rain, go away.

I want the sun to shine today.

I hear the thunder.

I feel the rain.

Do you think the sun
   will shine again?

The sun shines again
on a summer day.
We go on a picnic far away.
I talk to a butterfly, but he
is still too busy to talk to me.

Winter, spring, summer, fall,
I like summer best of all.
I go to the beach.
I play in the sand.
I jump in the waves
    far away from land.

I jump. I swim.

I float like a boat.

Sometimes the sea pushes me.

Sometimes it pulls me.

It pushes and pulls me all about

as I float like a boat,

floating in, floating out.

I can dig a big hole, deep and wide.
I can dig a big hole
    where crabs can hide
    after the water comes inside.

I can build a sand house
with shells for the floor,
shells for the windows,
the roof and the door.
Will my sandhouse stay
or wash away on a summer day?

I do like summer.
Will summer stay?
Will I come to the beach
   another day?
Will I have another holiday?
Why does summer go away?

Summer

Jane Belk Moncure

It's a hot, hot sum-mer day and I shall go a-way—— a-

way to the sand and the sea. Come with me! Splash in the waves,

dig in the sand. Sail in my boat far a-way from land.

Let's catch a whale or a crab will do, on a hot sum-mer day with you.